This Book Belongs To
Chris Frank

W9-ARU-578

p.47 Jonelle Beasley

p.47 Jessica West

p.66 Tyler Williams

ANTHOLOGY OF POETRY
BY
YOUNG AMERICANS®

2004 EDITION
VOLUME LXI

Published by Anthology of Poetry, Inc.

©*Anthology of Poetry by Young Americans*®
2004 Edition
Volume LXI

All Rights Reserved©

Printed in the United States of America

To submit poems
for consideration in the year 2005 edition of the
Anthology of Poetry by Young Americans®,
send to: poetry@asheboro.com or

> Anthology of Poetry, Inc.
> PO Box 698
> Asheboro, NC 27204-0698

Authors responsible
for originality of poems submitted.

The Anthology of Poetry, Inc.
307 East Salisbury • P.O. Box 698
Asheboro, NC   27204-0698

Paperback ISBN: 1-883931-46-0
Hardback ISBN: 1-883931-45-2

Anthology of Poetry by Young Americans®
is a registered trademark of
Anthology of Poetry, Inc.

It seems impossible that in 2004, a full fifteen years after the first publication of the *Anthology of Poetry by Young Americans*®, that we could be humbled, astonished, moved to tears and enlightened. It must be that we thought we had read it all; heard it all. And here, once again, we quietly learn that we continue to learn from the hearts and minds of this great nation's youth.

Within these pages you will find a marketplace of thought: Rich poems, rhythmic words, colorful imagery, sweet songs for our ears, nectar for our tongues, food for the hungry reader's heart and soul. Each page herein contains an offering, a satisfying meal for the mind prepared by a youthful writer who tilled the fertile grounds of creative thought and brought forth to us a ripened poem meant solely for our feast!

Now it is time to accept the invitation of our gentle hosts. Settle in, open up, and dine on free thought at a table prepared of unselfish giving. Enjoy the poems, savor each slowly, and marvel, as do we, at the masterful works of our enthusiastic young writers.

The Editors

DEAR PARENTS

I hid in the darkness,
until that one early morn,
when I entered the world,
that day I was born.

As an infant, I grew,
in a world full of care.
I was blessed with your love,
much more than was fair.

As I grew to a toddler,
you taught me good from bad.
And up to this day,
for that I am glad.

And I became a kid,
opening my eyes, thriving at school.
And I began to drift away,
your little jewel.

And now I am a teen,
spreading my wings, starting to fly.
You hold onto me, as much as you can,
but I get hard to hold onto, and you know why.

I'll continue to grow and progress,
first college, then a career,
but please remember this--
I'll always be yours, have no fear.

Grant L. Lin
Age: 13

Wolves are...
Caring to family things
Brave things
Fast, smart, misunderstood things-- skillful.

Wolves are...
Sweet things
Nice, harmless things-- lovable.

Wolves are...
Pack things
Valuable things
Loving, misunderstood-- helpful.

Wolves are...
Charming things
Special things
Endangered, small-numbered, pack hunters-- helpful.

Wolves are not...
Murdering things
Killing things-- bad.

But, wolves are... fine things
Hunted things
Trapped things
Slaughtered, eating, skinned things-- harmed.

Colte Elkin
Age: 9

Lying around
Taking in the summer sound
Knowing that I am school bound
Hoping that I won't be found.

James Coffey

THE BEST HOUR OF MY SUMMER

Playing in the sand and in and out of the water,
All the while, the weather is getting hotter.
Racing in the sand and leaving tracks,
And when that is over we decide to relax.

Abby Dye

TAKEN SO SOON

His life was taken so soon, so unexpectedly
no one wants this to happen to anyone
especially someone's young son.
Although since he's gone
it may hurt for a while
or it may hurt for a long time,
but never forget the good times you had with him,
even though thinking about the good times
may seem like it makes it hurt worse that he's gone,
the pain you feel, is not bad
it's just the joy that you had him,
and the time you spent with him,
never regret that you didn't do enough for him,
you most likely have done more than you will ever know.
Although you will never be with him physically again
he will always be around you in heart and mind,
you will one day again see him and live with him forever.

Sean P. Mahoney
Age: 18

AUTUMN DAYS

Wind is silently, steadily, blowing.
  The sky's so dark as if it's going to start snowing.
Outside, a squirrel is crawling.
  In a tree, a bird is cawing.
On this cold autumn day, everything is quiet,
  Very, very, very quiet.
Hurry up squirrel. Start gathering your acorns today,
  Or you're going to pay.
Hurry up bear, before it's too late.
  Be ready to lie down and hibernate.

Taylor Gray
Age: 10

LOVE

Love is bright pink and red
Tasting like a sweet lollipop
Smelling like roses in a flower shop
Like fireworks shooting off
A bird's song in your car
Someone caring about you!

Jordan Dora

LOVE

Love is a funny feeling,
if the one doesn't love you back!
You feel like you have let down a person,
not just any person, your best friend!
All of these feelings together are like madness,
not a good thing!
But yet love is in all of us,
a very powerful thing indeed!

Samantha Phillips

NON-KNIGHT

There once was a knight
Who didn't know how to fight
Her sword went up,
Her shield went down,
And she fell in a heap on the ground!

Elise Massicotte

MY SECRET

I looked down at my shoes to see if they were tied.
Teammates asked if I was nervous; I said no; I lied.
My stomach had butterflies, I had a headache.
My legs started to cramp, I began to shake.

I felt fatigued, worn, and run-down.
My figure was bent over, with a frown.
Nobody could know how much it hurt.
I felt like I was to get sick right there in the dirt.

I really don't know why I felt this way.
It was just a game, so I began to pray.
"Please help me do my very best.
Guide me through this challenging test.

"Assist me until all is over and done.
Comfort me when the battle is won.
No matter if the outcome is in favor or not.
Be there for me if I like it or not."

Suddenly a weight had been lifted from me.
God had listened, He heard my plea.
I then felt awesome, fabulous, and great.
All the pain I had felt seemed to evaporate.

I played the game and did very well.
My secret was this, which I am going to tell.
God knew my troubles and helped me through.
And if you ask Him, He will do the same for you.

Kurt C. Skaggs
Age: 14

CLIFFORD

Clifford is my cat,
He's really sort of fat,
He weighs twenty pounds,
and likes to dig mounds,
He buries his food with a towel,
And the other cat starts to growl,
He likes it when I'm home,
To brush him with his comb,
We like to play hockey,
Then my doll is his jockey,
He likes for me to scratch his ear,
While I tell him stories that I hear,
I like to sleep with him,
While the lights are dim,
I wouldn't trade Clifford for a million dollars,
Or even for a million collars,
Clifford is the bestest cat,
Even if he's really fat.

Jessica Blum
Age: 10

THE QUILT OF THE SMOKY'S

A shadow of gray velvet draped over a mountain
On top of a red, yellow, and orange patchwork quilt
Tall and graceful
Casting a shadow of magnificence on the valley below

A rushing river of water
A gift of the Smoky's
Only a stitch
In the Smoky's quilt of life

As the quilt goes on
Parts are added
And parts are lost
Each loss causes a sadness
Each gain as valuable as the next

As intricate as anything
A master seamstress could make
It goes on forever
In the Smoky's quilt of life

Millicent Cripe
Age: 10

Wolves are...
Handsome things
Graceful things
Gentle, loving, caring things-- loyal to pack.

Wolves are...
Fast things
Sly, observant things-- out of their dens.

Wolves are...
Misunderstood things
Brave things
Respectful, responsible-- alpha led.

Wolves are...
Working things
Depending things
Shy, scared, obedient-- around people.

Wolves are not...
Dimwitted things
Killing things-- evil.

But, wolves are...
Free things
Wild things
Cooperative things
Playful, teamworking, trustworthy-- family member.

Ian McDaniel
Age: 9

Wolves are...
Loving things
Courageous things
Graceful, beautiful, majestic things-- living.

Wolves are...
Fast things
Strong, meat-eating things-- adventurous.

Wolves are...
Hunted things
Hated things
Cunning, trapped by people things-- killed.

Wolves are...
Teamworking things
Responsible things

Wolves are not...
Bad things
Careless things-- killers.

But, wolves are...
Caring things
Teamworking things
Living things
Shy, working, brave-- respecting.

Stuart Combs
Age: 10

FRIENDS

Friends are like snowflakes on a winter day
All are unique in their very own way
When you're with a friend you're on an island
With an ocean of smiles and a sea of laughter

Friends are like leaves on a cool, autumn day
Each one different in their own, special way
When you're with a friend you're in heaven
Having the best time of your life

Friends are like flowers on a sunny, spring day
They're all so beautiful and oh, so much fun
When you're with a friend you're on an open field
Free to do anything, anytime, anywhere

Friends are like your shadow on a hot, summer day
They'll always stick with you, by your side forever

Carly Turner
Age: 11

LISTENING

Listen here while I mutter,
The butterflies in your stomach might flutter.
Listen to me use your mind,
Then maybe you will find,
These words I will speak to you,
"Hey"
you can speak them too.
Just like I do,
It'll be like life when it is new
Listen to me while I say
live your life just your way!

Jasmine White
Age: 10

AMAZING NATURE

A sunny and warm day
Beautiful at sunset
Birds, children, a soft wind breeze
Rides, people, amazing nature
Playing, getting fresh air, time with family
In spring, in summer, in fall of the year
Happy that I can frolic in the park.

Zara Anwarzai

VOLCANO

As I walked on the island,
And my toes hit the sand,
I noticed booming.
It was coming from a tall part of land.
When I saw the shadow of fire,
I began to wonder
If it was a volcano.

As my eyes saw the rocks falling,
I knew it was a calling.
I should not be here
Because the volcano is near.
The lava was spreading.
Home is where I was heading!

Vanessa Hamilton
Age: 11

WARM WATER

When the sun is shining high noon
The best time to see children
Splashing in water
Swimmers and divers in the neighborhood pool
Talking with friends
In June, July, and August
Feeling so wonderful in the warm water.

Elizabeth Batiuk

TIARA TIARA

Tiara, tiara,
  You are like a crown.
Tiara, tiara,
  You never let me down.

Tiara, tiara,
  Can't you see you will be so nice to me.

Tiara, tiara,
  You shine like a star.

Tiara, tiara,
  You are so bright.
You shine like the stars
  At night.

Kayleigh Sayers
Age: 11

JELL-O

You get the Jell-O from the box
You make it
You cook it
You take it out.

The Jell-O will be
Rubbery
Blubbery
Jiggly
Slimy
And cold.

You eat the colored,
Flavored
Jell-O
And it will
Slide
D
O
W
N
Your throat.

Alex Tichenor
Age: 10

PILLOWS

Pillows come in shapes
Like squares
And circles.

They are also in sizes
Like fat and small,
They can be tall.

They are cuddly, soft,
And fluffy
As you know...
They are used for sleeping.

Lorraine Kottka
Age: 11

SHOELACES

You can tie knots in shoelaces.
The strings sometimes trip you.
The string is on the shoe
Which is
On your foot.
The shoelaces have
Stripes
With colors.

Chase Marando

ICICLE

I want to find a big icicle.
They are wet and slimy.
I'd hit them against trees and rocks.
They are hard and cold.

I like to throw them.
I picked up an icicle and it slipped
Out of my hand.

I eat them.
I want to find a big icicle.

Kyle Logan Poort
Age: 11

JET

They fly high
In the sky.
They use amazing speed,
Speed like Mach 5.
It shoots its chain gun
While in a barrel roll.
They shoot missiles
To kill their opponent.
Then they dodge bombs to stay alive.

Curt Holt

STAR

There was once a star...
A movie star.
She was a cutie,
They called her Beauty.
She was always the hit of the show.

Once she made a pie
That baked up in the sky
And decided to lie.

When she comes to town
She holds her hair down and looks like a clown.

We thought, "Why is it going to fly?"
We called a spy whose name was Sly.
She found that every boy around
Was looking 'round at her.
Then she said, "I'm Ted."
She pulled off a wig and she looked like a pig!

Sarah West
Age: 10

WAITING

He waited in the dingy room of the hospital.
Desperately, he wanted relief from the horror--
No more sitting in the anteroom for hours.
Now the accident seemed miles away.

He had been reckless and crashed into a train,
It was only a race to see which was faster--
The car or the train.
His friend was in the back
And that was where the train hit.

He picked up a magazine, sang a song,
Did anything to pass the time.
Finally the doctor came out and lowered his eyes
And told him that his friend had just died.

Dennis J. Lee
Age: 16

ALL KINDS OF PEOPLE

People are very different.
No one is the same.
Some quietly do their work
While others get all the fame.

Some people are very smart,
But others barely get through school;
Some people just sit and read
While others act like they're so cool.

Some people are very fat;
Others are as thin as a stick.
Some people are very healthy
While others are always sick.

Some people have holes in their pockets;
Others spend money well.
Some people can keep your secrets,
But others always tell.

There are many more kinds of people than these.
I wonder which kind you are.
Whatever kind, you're special,
Though like one in a billion stars.

Katie Anderson
Age: 13

ODE TO A TAILGATE

On the corner of Fess and Thirteenth Street,
Where tall trees and parked cars form long straight lines,
The red-clad and gold-clad do meet and greet,
Sharing food and beverages of all kinds.
Some sit, some stand, throwing footballs about.
Rostered team players resisting a rout.
The music blares like a yelping bloodhound.
Heads bobbing, arms swaying, dancers abound.

Light slowly edges away from the fans,
Tables and chairs loaded back into vans.
Police on the prowl, lights flashing so bright,
Be careful; drive safely; driver tonight?
Away from the tailgate, cars in a fleet,
From the corner of Fess and Thirteenth Street.

Ali Nykiel

THE LIFTED LORAX

L ifted away to a better place
O nce-ler is stuck, all alone
R acing to save the trees by himself
A ngry that the truffula trees are destroyed
e X pected the once-ler to work out "unless"

Jack Judge

AROUND THE WORLD

Traveling the world is my big passion.
I love to go places just to plunder.
Myths of yore tell tales of wonder.
I'd love to see them, although they're ashen.
On London streets, I saw new fashion.
I saw sites of Don Quixote's blunder.
Arc de Triomphe is what I walked under.
In Las Vegas neon lights were flashin'.

So now as the bright sun winks like an eye,
The Pharaoh's tomb makes me want to cry.
All of history swarms around me.
I'm filled with ancient and modern culture.
The sun beats down my back like a vulture.
I've learned what beauty is meant to be.

Jessica Pleitner
Age: 17

SIZZLING SUMMER

These are some reasons
    Summer is my favorite season,
You can see a lot of animals walking around,
    And I really like animals
When I hear them make a sound.
You can swim in a pool,
    Which is really cool.
It is really hot and warm,
    Which is not really the norm.
You are off of school for two months or more,
    You can go to the beach or play at the shore.
So now you know my reasons
    I like summer better than other seasons!

Jessica Sinclair
Age: 11

DREAMS

Dreams are cool
    Dreams are sweet
Anything can happen
    When we are asleep
Tossing and turning all night long
    Dreaming up our own little towns
Fast asleep we lay in our beds
    Dreaming fast in our little heads

Alex Young

TRUTH

I am a spider spinning a thick web of lies
Lies that I weave and twist which become very mad
Finding out the truth to them would make people sad
The truth will soon come out like the sunrise
That light will make the scary black spider slowly die
The truth is finally out, which makes me really glad
But the people around me, they seem so very sad
Must be a comfort blanket and listen to their cries....

All of this will inevitably destroy many people's lives
Full of deceit, grief, hate, and pain are these lies
Once told they cannot be brought back or summoned
To tell one to a friend could mean the end
This extremely important message to you I must send
Never lie or you just might end up being condemned

Kristen Kendall

SMILES THE CLOWN

There once was a clown named Smiles
Who had a small hat and big shoes.
In the circus he learned many tricks
Like to juggle and play gazoos.

Smiles was a simple clown.
He liked farm animals.
He would feed each one
In their own special bowls.

Then one day he realized
He could join a show.
He already had the traits
And he already did know.

Then another day he tried out
To be a funny clown.
He already had a clown name
And he liked to travel from town to town.

He was hoping he could make it.
He knew he had a chance.
He even knew how
To do a little dance.

Smiles went on stage one day
To try out for a clown.
He stubbed his toe and tripped and fell.
And with him his hopes went down.

Then one day
All the results were in.
Smiles had made it,
So he began to grin.

Smiles was in the circus.
He had three days to get on the train.
And the day he left
It began to rain.

Smiles had a happy life
Performing some cool tricks.
But what he liked the most
Was getting elephant licks.

Matthew Staninger
Age: 12

ONCE-LER

O xygen matters not to the once-ler
N othing changes until a seed from the once-ler
C haos destroys nature with the once-ler
E arth suffers from greed
L ife without a good ecosystem
E mpties away the plants, animals, and people
R ecycle the world and speak for the trees.

Arne Sorenson

TURKEY

I'm hunting for a turkey.
Thanksgiving is coming up.
My family is waiting for food on the table.
I see a turkey. It's nice and plump.
I aimed my gun then I realized,
Should I sacrifice a life for mine?
I came home with my hands empty.
But in my pocket were ears of corn.
I told my family the story.
They all said, "I'm proud of you for letting a turkey live."

Leslie Peterson
Age: 11

THIS IS THE WAY
MY FOSTER GRANDPARENT READS

This is the way my foster grandparent reads to me
And I feel like I'm really in the story
I love her expression in her voice
It makes me think and feel that I am in a play
In front of many people
She hugs me when she reads
And sometimes makes up her stories
This is the way my foster grandparent reads.

Jessica Diego

HAPPY THE CLOWN

There was a clown named Happy,
he was so happy he was flippy flappy.
One day the circus came to town,
he decided to be the clown.
He walked up on stage,
all scared and afraid.
But his head held high,
it almost touched the sky.
He did his part,
it was very smart.
He climbed on a ladder,
and jumped in a platter.
It made a big mess,
he had no stress.
Everyone laughed
because what Happy did after.
He ran around stage
like one big parade.
Now Happy the clown is a big hit.
Whenever they see his name in big print,
they jump with glee
and yell "Hee hee."
Happy is a big hit
he'll be the best one I have ever met.

Brittni Moles
Age: 12

LOVE

Love.
Love is a strong thing.
As strong as hard rain.
Love is kindness to the heart.
Love never ends but it starts.
That's what love is.

Kayelin Raechel Martens
Age: 9

MY NIGHT FRIGHT

Owls hooting in the park.
Monsters hiding in the dark.
It's very very, very, very, unbelievably scary!
My night fright is the scariest fright I ever had!
I tried to wake up my dad.
But when I did it was very bad!
He was a monster who knew how to torture!
When this all happened it was a scorcher!
When I realized I was dreaming.
I woke up and saw a monster beaming!

Ashley Faucault

CHRISTMAS

Christmas! Oh, Christmas!
I love Christmas.
The presents.
The cheer.
People shopping.
Hanging stockings.
People play in the snow.
Let's have a racc.
Go! Go! Go!
To the snow!
Snow! Snow!
Let's decorate the tree!
The Christmas tree!
Oh, the presents, the holly!
I love Christmas!

Alexandria Macias
Age: 8

THE JOURNEY OF BUBBLEGUM AND SAPPHIRE

There once was a girl named Bubblegum.
Who was as skinny as a crumb.
Each day she ate one pea.
That's how she became so tiny.
Bubblegum also liked monkeys.
She said they reminded her of her Grandma Clonkies.
Bubblegum had a pet monkey named Sapphire.
Sapphire hated to sit around a campfire.
One time Sapphire saw one,
And started screaming, "Run, run, run."
Bubblegum's mom got tired of it.
So she shouted, "Make that monkey quit!"
She also said, "Make that monkey a stray."
Bubblegum got so mad, she decided to run away.
She packed a suitcase full of peas and monkey pictures.
And for some odd reason, she packed cupcake mixtures.
Bubblegum and Sapphire ran away
to a place called Hackelbestalors.
There they became pro sailors.
The only food they ate was peas and cupcakes.
So now all they have is really big stomachaches.
Now they are smart and are heading home.
And now I'm going to end this poem.

Emily J. Mastej
Age: 12

HELLO

I said hello to a stranger that went by,
They had a sort of glare in their eye.
It seemed as though it was something I said,
Or maybe the person just got out of bed.

It just seems so strange, someone getting mad,
Just from a word or conversation they had.
It's probably because no one says hi,
They ignore each other as they walk by.

I don't understand this concept at all, though
I mean, what's so bad about saying hello?
It's not like it takes up too much of your time,
And it's not like you're committing some sort of crime.

If people said hello in this world more,
I'm sure everyone wouldn't be so sore.
So the next time you pass someone in a bad mood,
Stop and say hi with a good attitude.

Cassi Polster
Age: 12

CRAZY CARL

Carl is a crazy man.
He lives pickled in a can.
He doesn't like publicity.
He lives just outside the city.
He hates other beings
And despises all his feelings.
Carl is a crazy man
Who lives pickled in a can.

Andrew Griggs
Age: 11

BASEBALL

B alls flying out of the park
A ll of the crowd screaming out loud
S inging "The National Anthem" before every game
E very pitch is a ball or a strike
B allplayers take the field
A ll the balls getting thrown about
L eaving the field depressed, the fans are
al L of 'em sad because their team lost

Jim O'Donnell

PEACE AND WAR

There are two trails to choose to follow
In this time of peril.
These two paths are opposites;
One of peace and one of war.

The path to war is an easy one;
Anyone may take it.
Yet in the end what turns out
Is truly horrifying.

People destroying others;
Complete annihilation.
In the end, the easy way
Is not easy or right.

The way to peace is difficult
But pleasant when taken.
No one dies and life goes on
As it would normally.

I have chosen the path of peace.
Will you follow me?

Rastko Ciric
Age: 11

APOCALYPSE

As darkness approaches,
The lines of battle form.
As darkness approaches,
Flames shoot through the sky.
As darkness approaches,
The war bursts forth with utter chaos.

Apocalypse, Apocalypse,
The end draws near.

As the heavens darken,
The ground is shattered.
As the heavens darken,
Time warps into disorder.
As the heavens darken,
The world is thrust into black flames.

Apocalypse, Apocalypse,
The end is here.

The very fabric of space
Becomes shattered shards of energy...

Apocalypse has struck.

Strahinja Ciric
Age: 10

CATS JUST CATS

Tigers are neat,
They like meat.

Cheetahs have spots,
Like a Dalmatian's dots.

Panthers are black,
Like a Halloween cat.

Cougars are brown,
Just like a brownie.

The other animals,
Run from the lion lying in the sun.

Cats go purr,
When you pet their fur.

But kittens are the cutest
Then the rest.
Their rough tongue
On your cheek
Says the words
They cannot speak.

Megan Cox
Age: 8

SORROW

You're in the hospital, feeling blue.
　You've got many visitors who want to see you.
You're lying in bed, not doing too good,
　You wanna go home, you wish you could.
There are doctors and nurses surrounding you,
　Going in for surgery, but nothing you can do.
I miss you a lot, and I want you here.
　So I sent you this poem to put in some cheer.
The hospital may smell really quite bad.
　Sick people moaning, feeling so sad.
The food tastes queer, not good at all,
　But when you get home you'll have a ball.
These are tough situations, you'll make it through.
　I believe you can, 'cause you always do.

Dedicated to John Novath (open-heart surgery) 11/2003

Cassandra E. Polster
Age: 12

DROPLET

Many raindrops,
Big and small,
Fresh and clean.
Do you know how many fall?

Billions and trillions,
All made of water, quickly, forever.
Just a small gift from God,
Should WE waste it? Never!!

A single droplet,
Small and wet.
Can you catch one on your tongue?
Yeah? Well, that's a bet!

Mandy Bishop
Age: 10

SHE'S AN ANGEL

She is an angel. Do you know who?
Well, I will tell you once I am through.
When she stayed with us, she would use my room.
We would go for breakfast, and have lunch at noon.
I can still hear her laughter and smell her scent.
Thanksgiving and Christmas are the times we spent.
I love her very much, and I know she loves me.
I keep imagining her hugging me so lovingly.
Now I will tell you who, what, and when
She was truly an angel, my Auntie Helen
She left us when I was just seven.
And now she is up in Heaven.
She is made of kindness, she is made of love.
And now she watches over me from above.

In loving memory of Auntie Helen

Christine Lewandowski
Age: 12

I AM THANKFUL

I am thankful for my family.
Mom is gold.
Dad is silver.
T. J. is blue.
The color of my family is red the color of love.
Why is my mom gold?
She makes the money in the family.
Why is my dad silver?
He takes care of T. J. and I.
Why is T. J. blue?
He plays with me.
Why is red the color of my family?
It's the color of love... Thank you!

Alexa Schiller
Age: 8

MY CERTAIN SOMEONE

I know a certain someone who always makes me smile.
And that certain someone always drives me wild.
That certain someone never makes me frown.
I think that certain someone is the best in the town.
That little certain someone is always there for me.
I'll go anywhere for that person,
even if I have to cross the sea.

Alex Kessler

MY DREAM

I sat and thought about the dream I had.
Parts were happy parts were sad
I heard shouting and laughter all over the place
Crying and tears on somebody's face.

Yet in my dream who could this stranger be?
This mystery person, looking at me
I stepped back and looked and saw it again
This mystery person was really my friend.

The dream was ending and fading away
I hope my friend has found peace today!

Emily Markovich
Age: 13

GO FALL GO

I was flying my kite.
My friend did a sigh.
Whoo I smell pie.
Mr. Gregor was drinking Pepsi.
The leaves were falling off the tree.
By the time you know it my brother was three.
My mom opened the door.
By the time you know it I was four.

Allan Austin III

SEASONS

Winter, spring, summer, fall,
the truth is God made them all.
Seasons change through time,
that is why I made this rhyme.
When winter comes and January's here,
snow comes down and spring is near.
Spring is here... yes! Oh my!
That flower's touching to the sky!
Summer's a time when you swim in pools...
that is why summer rules!
When fall is here and leaves drop,
the farmer restores the crop!
Winter, spring, summer, fall,
the truth is God made them all!

Jessica Hunt
Age: 8

MY COUSIN IS A SCAREDY-CAT

My cousin is a scaredy-cat. She is afraid of the night.
She has to sleep with a light.
She sleeps with a bat that looks like a rat.
When she is around kites her face turns white.
When she screams her face turns green.

Alyssa Michelle Anderson

IF I

If I find you in my room,
I would say,
Take the broom,
If I caught you in the rain,
I would say,
You have a better brain,
If you don't share,
I would say,
Act like you care,
If I caught you in the road,
I would say,
Go catch a toad!!!

Hayley Morris
Age: 9

THE PRINCIPAL'S OFFICE

The principal's office is what you say,
children are in it all day.
If you find that you have never been there one time,
if you go in there you see your parents' faces,
you're in trouble!
So I'll warn you, be good!

Jessica Bunch

I WISH, I WISH

I wish, I wish, I had a pet fish,
I would name the fish, Swish,
He wold go in my bedroom,
On top of a gold dish,
But I can only wish for a pet fish.

I wish, I wish I could touch a star,
I try to jump up really far,
I know I can't reach it in a car,
So I try to catch it in a jar,
But I can only wish to touch a star.

I want to have gazillion birthdays,
I want to have my own rules and ways,
I want to have a lot of pet blue jays,
But I can only dream and wish,
For all these things,
I wish, I wish!

Allison K. Schroeder

HELP

I need your help through it all
to kiss my scratches when I fall.
Today will be the end of all.

So help me when the pain is burning;
for your love I wait, I'm yearning.

Softest grip, it's you I pick.
There's not one thing you can't fix.

Help me break this wall down,
so I don't look like such a clown.

Help me when this clock starts ticking.
Hands are squeezing, legs are kicking.

Help me when my love is drowning,
even when my heart is pounding.

Hold me now and hold me then.
Swear I'll never hurt again.
Help me make the sky curve in,
Then write my name on crystal skin.

No matter what you help me do,
I swear, I'll always think of you.

Jessica Otto
Age: 13

TEACHERS

Teachers, teachers everywhere.
Here and there and everywhere.
Going shopping,
Teaching kids.
Teachers are so awesome and cool!

Jonelle Beasley

MY BROTHER JUSTIN

I love my brother Justin,
He plays sports all the time.
He gets double breakfast on Fridays
Paying with nickels and dimes.
Justin gets straight A's in every subject including math.
He always does his homework after his bath.
I love Justin from head to toe,
But he will always know
That I love him brother or not.
HE'S THE BEST BRO I KNOW!

Jessica West

NO ONE SEES IT IN MY EYES

You don't know how I'm feeling
I have no courage to vocalize
These camouflaged emotions
Have immobilized my words
No one sees it in my eyes

I long to tell you how much I love you
But I'm frightened of your reply
Embarrassed like a little girl
No one sees it in my eyes

I tremble when I am near you
Deep desire in disguise
Chills travel throughout my body
But no one sees it in my eyes

I wipe my tears of emptiness
Although the pain will never die
My wounded heart won't ever heal
But you'll never see it in my eyes

Megan Komp
Age: 12

THE JAG

The car was the love of my life, that beast.
I drove it with pride and bathed it often.
I would wash it, like, like once a day, at least,
but then on black ice it met its coffin.

One morn I was cruising en route to school
Wish I had known the weather was freezing.
Across the yellow I could see the fool
drifting to my lane, a sight not pleasing.

I swerved, now slamming the brake to the floor,
Missed the van but not the curb, fence, or tree.
Air bag deployed I got out in horror,
my face got cut up, the car worse than me.

The cop wasn't cool but I wasn't fined.
I'll have the roadster forever in mind.

Jay Lucas

SEASONS

Summer, spring, winter, and fall.
Those are the seasons and I like them all.
In winter you get to throw snowballs.
And in the fall well,
I don't think you get to throw anything at all.
My name is Cloe and I am going to say
that I love all the seasons just the same way.
Summer, spring, winter, and fall.

Cloe Carda
Age: 8

Dear Misery,
You have imprisoned me
And yet...
You have set me free
Into a world filled with hatred and deceit
Please, Misery,
I beg of you...
Remember me when I am gone
For I no longer need your company.
Good-bye.

Andrea Arndt

WHAT THE WORLD HAS COME TO

When the ground starts shaking
And the bombs start breaking
The world is no longer at peace

When the bullets are flying
And the body count's rising
Will these wars ever cease?

Over and over we hear about Americans dying overseas
It brings people all over the world
   crumbling to their knees
To what is this amounting
Because the death toll keeps counting
Troops get sent all over the earth
The guns are still smoking
There's no time for joking
Just think about it, what is this worth.

Jon Brown

THINGS I DON'T KNOW

I don't know where the remote is.
I don't know where my belt went.
I don't know who took my backpack.
I don't know what happened to my basketball uniform.
I don't know where my water bottle is.
I don't know where I left my coat.
I don't know who took my backpack.
I don't know where the cordless phone went.
I don't know where my gym clothes went.

I, ESPECIALLY, DON'T KNOW
HOW THEY ALWAYS SEEM TO JUST SHOW UP.

Drew Dennis
Age: 12

FAILURE

Do you know that saying?
Failure is not an option?
Failure is not an option!
Failure, is NOT an option!
Well, failure is only a fear, a state of mind,
That can easily be overcome by doing your very best
And I have learned to overcome that fear
By the help of my many friends,
And I thank them for that.

Andrew Peckat

FRIENDS

I have many friends, as you may or may not see.
Some live close, and some are very far away from me.
But friends mean the same.
A friend is someone who can say "lean on me,"
And have an open shoulder for you to see.
Someone who cares,
Someone who loves me,
Someone who can take my problems,
Let them go, and set them free!
They make me feel confident and good inside.
They can wipe my tears when I want to cry.
They make me feel happy; I feel like I could fly.
Why I have such awesome friends,
I could only wonder why.
I see them as a blessing God has kindly granted me.

Amber Maguire
Age: 14

SILLINESS

Bouncy and fun,
do a ton,
round-offs and flips,
touch your own hips.
I don't know what this is,
but I think it is silliness.

Margaret Knutsen

CLASS OF 2004

Class of 2004,
I will miss and love you forevermore.
As we say our good-bye,
We try not to cry,
But the tears just pour and pour.

As we go our separate ways,
Sometimes we'll sit in a daze.
We'll remember the good times and bad,
And sometimes even the sad.
How we will long for those junior high days.

We've been through a lot together,
And wish we could stay there forever.
But as we all know,
To high school we must go.
But this class we will always remember.

As I said before,
I will always miss and love you forevermore.
I hope we can keep in touch,
And hold our friendship with a strong clutch.
Class of 2004.

Kristen Bohling
Age: 14

FRIEND OR FOE

People say there's a difference between a friend and a foe
A friend will make you laugh
A foe will make you cry
A friend will make you happy
A foe will make you sad
A friend will help you up
A foe was one who tripped you
But when things all add up
There isn't really a big difference
When a friend betrays you your foe is there
When you get to know your foe he's really very nice
Although you may feel like there is no one there
If you look around there is always a friend or foe
Waiting to help

Sarah Marie Fry
Age: 12

Why are people so unhappy with themselves?
So unhappy that they feel they have to change
Have to change so that they can fit in
Why do people put these thoughts in their heads?
Why can't a person just be who they are?
Be true to yourself
Do what you want
Do it because it's right for you
Not because you feel that you have to
And let yourself shine through

Sarah Hilbrich

THE SHOE

Have you ever heard the saying,
  "if the shoe doesn't fit...?"
Well when I met you , it didn't one bit.
My foot was too small to fit in the shoe
It didn't seem a best friend relationship
  could happen between us two.
After hanging out for days,
We became alike in so many different ways.
My foot began to grow,
And so did our friendship, ever so slow.
Being famous together is our dream,
Shining like a star, we will beam.
Over time, the shoe was the perfect size,
This came to me as quite a surprise.
When I think about my foot fitting the shoe,
I'm so glad I became best friends with you!!

Dominique Anne Frankovich
Age: 12

SPLISHY THE FISHY

I have a fishy,
His name is Splishy,
He likes to swim around his dishy.
His dishy is round,
It has rocks on the ground,
And a plant in the middle that's swishy.

Katherine L. Engel

WHO AM I?

I am called huge by all
Although in person I am small.
I run and run
Until the game is done.

When the game begins
We already deserve the win
Don't come in my corner
'Cause I'll run you over.

Twenty-five is my number
I would pick no other
When the runner comes with the ball
He is going to fall.

I have a big heart
And that is the best part
To know me is to love me
Just don't be on the other team.

Alex Matushek
Age: 13

GRADUATION DAY

Graduation day is the day I will not say good-bye
Some of us may be happy, while others may cry
We've been together for many special years
Now leaving the people I grew up with brings tears

Since we were little kids and now having to grow up
Although we've been through many hard times,
We cannot forget the good times

We mustn't forget the memories that we've shared
Or the many people that have always been there
  and cared
Our teachers have watched and helped us grow
Teaching us the things we must know

Graduation day is one of the saddest days of our lives
It is when we will all have to say our good-byes
It is when we will go our separate ways
But always remembering our younger days

These many years together I have hardly any regrets
All I know is I've been truly blessed
Never forget these moments
  once you walk out our school door
I will always remember and love you, class of 2004

Erica Martin
Age: 14

MY FAMILY THANKSGIVING

The girls look at carnations
And Thanksgiving decorations
The boys play football and no one gets hurt
But that doesn't count a rip in your shirt.

The women in the kitchen, and the men in the hall
When dinner is ready they will call

Before we eat we say a prayer
There are a few things we need to share
Laughter in the air and we're stuffing our faces
If you look around there is love in many places

Patrick Gorny
Age: 13

BUTTERFLIES

I saw a pretty butterfly
And I wondered why
Why they float so high
Up in the deep blue sky.
They were floating without a care
Up in the clean crisp air.
They have nothing to worry about...
I wish I were there.

Katie Skura

A BENCH

There is a bench in the corner of a park,
That is closed after dark.
When the guard locks up the gate,
It will not be opened until eight.

It is finally morning,
And the sun shines with glory.
As those iron doors break,
A man picks up a rake.

As he picks up the leaves,
There is pain in his knees.
He is searching for comfort,
And finds a great find.

A bench in the corner,
Is a great honor.
As he walks to the corner,
With a smile on his face.

Approaching the bench,
The leaves become dense.
As he picks up a leaf,
He falls down as to plea.

For the bench is so near,
But he has great fear.
That this unreachable bench,
Is not in his clench.

But as the day drawls,
He receives no applause.
For all he wanted was to rake up the leaves,
But no one is there to hear his drifting pleas.

But this he is certain,
As the guard is to close the iron curtain.

He will see this poor old man covered in leaves,
Under the trees.
Next to the bench,
With the unreachable clench.

And help the poor old man to his feet,
The old man would tell him his tale of his bad knee.
But as night drew near,
The guard still could not hear.

As he locked up the gate,
The man was stuck there 'til eight.
As the man recaptured his thoughts,
It all ended up in the bench's lap.

For the man was in pain,
He just wanted a rest.
Now he could rest on the cold wet ground,
And have dreams of benches going around.

He tried to grab hold but fell down so hard,
The man was lost forever.
Just another leaf in the air.

Kristin Walker
Age: 13

A DAY OF SCHOOL

Going to school is great,
  Imagine the things to create!
When recess gets out of control,
  Conflict managers go on patrol.
Whenever you don't get out of whack,
  Your teacher may give you a snack.
You have to earn field trips,
  And when we do, we feel to shake our hips.
Sometimes it's fun to learn,
  But it's no fun when bad luck gives you an F for a turn.
And sometimes you forget your Box Tops,
  And you remember too late
  and may give yourself bops.
Sometimes you see in classrooms desks and chairs,
  In nice and neat big pairs.
Now everyone likes recess,
  And when we get out, we say, "Yes!"
And when we learn some math,
  We continue the learning path.
When we work on tests,
  We always do our best.
And we all need a rest,
  When at school, we do our best.
And when you go to school,
  Then we know you aren't a fool.

Bennett Sanders
Age: 10

62

MY ANTELOPE

My antelope
He eats a lot of cantaloupe,
I said "why don't you try something new."
"But I'm am antelope
I'm supposed to eat cantaloupe"
One day he overloaded
Rumble Rumble Rumble Boom
He exploded!!!

When he died
Of course we all cried
I'm always alone
You can tell by my tone.
Then one day
I'm so happy to say
He's back he's back
Of course you know
When he came back
My hungry antelope
Wanted some more cantaloupe

Victoria P. Villaseñor
Age: 10

SOCCER

Let me tell you this story short
Soccer is my favorite sport

I wear a blue uniform
I keep it in my locker
It is always ready
With it on I feel calm and steady

Forward is my best position
It has a lot of competition

I wear Nike soccer shoes
With them on I'm sure I won't lose

Now I have my uniform and spiky shoes on
And run to the field with my teammate John

The referee, the whistle he blows
Into my ears the sound flows

I kicked the ball and began to run
I have to admit that it is fun

Someone hit John and they got a foul
The people in the stands began to howl

We had halftime and it passed
We had to drink very fast

The game started we began to play
Then I got the ball and with me it'll stay

I ran down the field, got ready to shoot
The fans on the sidelines got ready to hoot

I shot the ball and it went in
Right at the moment I thought we did win

On the weekends I wake up and say
Brother, brother wake up and play
Soccer, soccer for the rest of the day

Ahmad Aljobeh
Age: 10

MY FRIEND

My friend isn't fat,
She has a pet cat.
She is really good at tae kwon do,
I'm not jealous so I say, "So."
She has a bunk bed in her room,
She loves to look at the moon.

She goes to Jonas E. Salk,
She likes to draw pictures with chalk.
She knows my nickname is Ky,
We never ever want to say "Bye."

Kylee Stanko

A RACE AT MARTINSVILLE

A race at Martinsville is very crowded
People get food before the race so it's crowded.

It gets loud when the race starts,
Also when the train comes.

The track is the size of a mile
There's a wreck every once in a while.

The race is five hundred miles long,
So they race five hundred laps.

Gary Taylor
Age: 9

PIE

Hi, my name is Ty.
I like pie that I can buy.
If it's green, mean, teen,
Sad, mad, glad,
Fat or flat.
I, Ty, will buy that pie.

Ty Williams

THANKSGIVING

Thanksgiving is a thankful time of the year.
Thanksgiving is a time to give a great cheer!
At this thankful time of the year
We give out peace and good deeds.
Thanksgiving is a time to eat
Turkey and mashed potatoes.
It is also a time to celebrate
That the Pilgrims and the Indians
Joined together to have a big feast!
So we have a feast with our families.
I like this idea because we can be with our families.

Andrea Spencer
Age: 9

PEOPLE

There are people all around us
Here and there and there and here
There are people everywhere
People at the supermarket
People at the hardware store
People on the streets
No matter where they are
They are still people

Jim Loveless

PEACE

Peace. It sounds so beautiful,
Yet so far to reach for humankind.
Peace. The glue that holds us together,
Yet so far to reach for the human mind.

Peace, love, unity, that is we all need.
Wars, battles, bloodshed,
That is what we should not have.
Family and friends, that is what I give thanks for.
Food and shelter, that is why I give thanks.

There are many good people who do worthy things,
But there are many bad people who do devilish things.
They steal your money, jewelry, and even your family.
I am glad there are mostly good people in my town,
Their faces hardly ever have frowns.

There are many peaceful people in our society,
But some people are not.
Those people are corrupt.
Those people are thieves, murderers, bandits,
And even homicidal maniacs.
All those people should be caught.

Peace is what people wish and want,
But do we really need it?
Yes, of course!
Because evil is a really deep pit,
And at the bottom there are razor-sharp spikes.

If you want peace you should just be friendly,
And do not be hateful,
Just smile,
And once in a while,
Think of the family and friends
That gave you joy every day.

Tony Mannia

FOOTBALL

Football is my favorite sport
even if it's not played on court.
First you have to practice before you make the punt.
Then you better run because this next part won't be fun.
So don't look around
or you'll be on the ground.
Try to find the yellow poles
so you can make your team a field goal.

Kyle A. Linsemeyer
Age: 10

AMERICA

United States of America,
The red, white, and blue.
Stars and stripes on the flag,
It's all very true.
There are fifty states,
And Washington D.C.
America the beautiful,
The land of the free.
Before September 11th,
U. S. was a happier place.
There were two tall buildings,
Now ashes are in their place.
Many more people were alive.
Now they are missing and wanting to survive.
Everyone has been affected,
Deep down inside.
It's brought us all together,
And now we have great pride!

Ashley Martin

MY COUSIN'S CATS

My cousin's cats
  looked very fat.
Until they got a haircut.
  No, they did not look like a mutt.
Their names are Dude and Riley.
  They are not very smiley.
I don't know if they like meat.
  I do know they're neat.
They are both boys.
  They do not play with toys.
They go up in the attic.
  Their fur gets full of static.
My cousins put Dude in the baby stroller.
  The stroller has never fallen over.
Those are some facts
  about my cousin's cats.

Elizabeth Ufer
Age: 9

JUST ACROSS THE MILE

Distance is the space between,
Where glory stands, dividing dreams.
Cause to travel all the while,
And finally cross that dreaded mile.

It takes more will than time to race,
Across the lonely desert's face.
Where one's goal starts, another's ends,
Where one path runs straight, another bends.

It matters not where you begin,
Your destination lies within.
Despite the rugged trail you run,
You'll be there once your trek is done.

So do not fear the starting line,
When you are ready, meet the sign.
Keep safe with you a heart well spent,
And at the end, a soul content.

Chris A. McCoin
Age: 14

DESTINY

A lonely man walks by the moon,
It's full of detailed splendor
The moon eases his soul from its protective shell,
His spirit quietly surrenders
The light casts a shadow of something nearby,
He can feel its radiant glow
The shadow belongs to that of a woman,
His blood begins to quickly flow
Upon seeing her face he begins to feel weak,
Because her beauty has no compare
She must be an angel sent from above,
Because his heart melts with only a stare
The two finally touch,
He sheds only a single tear
He then knows she is there for him,
Which erases all his fears
If only one wish he had,
He would know exactly what to do
He would freeze this moment forever,
Under the light of the moon
The two stay together,
He knows he has been blessed
All their actions are for one another,
None of them are suppressed
Their love is forever,
Not intending to end soon
All of this happened,
Because of the light of the full moon

Glen A. Batista
Age: 17

THE PIG NAMED MATT

There was a pig named Matt
Who was most certainly fat
When everyone came to see the pig
He would usually hide under his mat
While everyone yelled "The fat pig Matt!"
So now you see that the pig named Matt
Was so lonely, very picky,
And always hid under his mat.
That is all about the fat pig named Matt.

Jake Hidalgo
Age: 10

FANTASIES

Fantasies are like dreams
Dreams are like thoughts
Thoughts are the future
And the future is me
Me is me and will always be
But what shall there be without thoughts and dreams?
One big fantasy

Marissa Hulpa

SEPTEMBER 11TH

September 11th is a day we will never forget
It has filled our hearts with great regret
On this day there was an attack
The skies changed quickly from blue to black
To everyone it was a surprise
We all couldn't believe our eyes
The two buildings quickly went down
Everyone's face was in a frown
To know the buildings are no more
To know families will now grow poor
On this day we all came together
Our nation suddenly grew better
We prayed for the ones we have now lost
And for their families it was the ultimate cost
This is a day that will remain in our hearts forever
And will still be a threat now and forever

Marcie Hulpa

TURTLES

Turtles live in the ocean and have lots of fun.
They play crabball like basketball.
They eat plants and swim all day.
Turtles don't have any predators
so they don't worry so much about tomorrow.
They hibernate in the winter and wake up in the summer.

Shannon Abraham
Age: 10

WAITING FOR YOU

Here I am waiting for you,
  I hope you're waiting for me too.
As I look to you from down here on the ground,
  I feel your love all around.
It's like someone is surrounding me,
  holding me, loving me, making me happy.
I'd never want to run or quake in fear,
  because I know that you are near.
I feel happy when I think of you,
  because you're mine forever true.
You're like a king in the throne,
  who loves his subjects to the bone.
You're like a mother bear,
  who guards her babies with so much care.
And when you look at me to see what I do
  I will be waiting just for you.

Azunne Anigbo

MILITARY

A rmy,
B ombs are deadly,
C arry weaponry,
D ead soldiers,
E ntry attack,
F -16s,
G uns,
H eavy artillery,
I njury from bombs,
J oint forces,
K ill enemies,
L ure into trap,
M arines,
N avy,
O peration of weapons,
P lanes,
Q ualify for military,
R escue,
S tealth bomber,
T anks,
U nits,
V isual of enemies,
W eaponry systems,
X XX,
Y ards of battlefield,
Z yrode of a weapon.

Aaron Lovall
Age: 10

FIRE AND RESCUE

They risk their life
to save someone like me.
I know when I need them,
they would be there day or night
to risk their life for you and me.
They are the best as you can see,
so I thank the fire and rescue
for putting their life at risk
to help save people like me.

Corey Igras
Age: 12

FRIENDS

Friends are there until the end
They'll never forget you in good times and bad
They always stick up for you when others don't

Friends stand together
Because no one can stand alone
Hand in hand friends will never be apart

So be a friend today
And help someone find the right way

Danielle Frankovich

SOMEONE SPECIAL TO ME

Someone special to me,
Is important you see.
When I was young,
We would play and have fun.
We would watch TV,
And sing to AC/DC.
I would sit on his lap,
While he was hard at work.
We would wash the car,
And do yard work.
This special person to me,
Loves and cares for me.
This special person to me,
Is my uncle I love to see.
My uncle is special to me,
He is important don't you see?

Megan M. Egert

SPACE

In space it looks so fun
You get a better look at the sun
No aliens trust me
It's as safe as can be

No lions, tigers, or bears
Just planets, but no chairs
You won't see months like May
One good thing is you don't have to pay

Nine planets you will find
Colors of all different kinds
In space there is no air
So humans couldn't bear

Are you worrying you might get tired up there
Because there are no chairs
But there is no gravity there
You have to worry about the air

Morgan Sandelski
Age: 9

BUNNY

Think of fall and think of a bunny.
Yes a bunny!

Their tail is thick, fluffy, and white
just like the fall clouds in their flight.

Their small round brown eyes
are like the acorns falling from the sky,
leaving their surprise.

The youthful, untamed bunny
is like the fallen leaves dancing in the wind,
how cunning, the bunny!

Jennifer Rose Van Oort

THE DAY I AM A BRIDE

I dream to be a bride
And seen worldwide
I will not hide
I will have lots of pride
Then step outside
And horseback ride.

Angela Hammond

BEFORE I FELL ASLEEP

Before I fell asleep, I saw him pray.
Before I nodded off I heard the Savior say,
"Let this cup pass over, if in Thy will."
Even though he was the Christ, he was humbled and still.

Before I fell asleep, soldiers came with many a sword.
Before I nodded off, they captured my Lord.
I was in a blind rage, "Kill," is all I could hear.
Without any thinking, I cut off a soldier's ear.

Before I fell asleep, they tore Jesus' back.
Before I nodded off, I heard the nine-tails crack.
Blood spewed from his body, so pure, so clean.
They didn't even know that he was the Holy King.

Before I fell asleep, I heard him cry,
"Father I give up, now I will die!"
Wherever his is forever, him I will keep.
Maybe I'll see him return before I fall asleep.

Trent E. Wilson
Age: 15

SCHOOL

School is a field,
a vast open field.
Students are wheat,
a golden ocean of plants
blowing in the wind.
Each year at harvest
they're cut down.
Some are traded
to better fields.
Most are replanted.
Some grow taller than others.
Some are for bread,
to feed the richest of the rich
to the poorest of the poor.

Garret Goodwin
Age: 13

STRANGER

There is a stranger in my wall
that stranger is very tall,
he always walks up and down the hall,
and follows me to the mall,
he helps my dad reach his saw
and helps my mom sew her shawl.
That stranger is my friend.

Becca Ripley

MY DOG

I have a dog,
Who looks like a hog.
He likes the fog.
He eats frogs.
He likes to jog on a big fat log.
He can swallow whole a big troll.
He can roll up a big, tall pole.
I love my dog.
He's such a hog.

Christine Hielkema
Age: 8

LONELINESS

L ove
O ut the door
N o shoulder to cry on
E mpty inside
L oyal friend
I llness
N o one to call for help
E ach friend gone
S afe no longer
S adness

Danielle Gilbert

FALL

You rake leaves into a great big pile
Then you jump into it with a great big smile
That's not all
You can do in the fall
You can play catch with your dog
Or ride your bike in the fog
But best of all it's my birthday
and my name is Kay
I walk into the house
I can't hear a mouse
The lights are out
Seven o'clock about
But to my surprise
Before I realize
HAPPY BIRTHDAY!
All I can say is
Thank you for everything

Kay Starzynski

FREEDOM

Freedom is what we stand for
Every American has it in their core
To others, it can be a big thing
Because they have to obey a king.

To Americans it is what we are
We fight for it in war
We stand up for it no matter what
While others stand against us.

To others, it may be nothing
But to me, it's a great something.

Kaitlin Schneider
Age: 12

MY CAT DELILA

My cat is black and white.
She meows a lot.
She scratches you a lot.
Her name is Delila.
She likes wet food.
She sleeps in our bathroom.
She is the best cat ever.

Jacinda Myers

A DAY AT THE BEACH

One day I went to the beach.
I was close enough to the water,
That it seemed at an arm's reach.

Sometimes I lay in the sun,
And sometimes I had a little fun.
It was that kind of day,
That all you could do was run.

When grabbing something to eat,
I would be taking a little break.
Then I would get done,
And take a dip in the lake.

But as the day grew dim,
I decided to take a swim.
The greatest way to end a day,
Is in that kind of way!

Ryan Slager

BILLY THE CLOWN

There once was a clown named Billy
He always told jokes and acted Silly
He got paid a lot
Had a costume with spots
And had a little dog named Willy.
He loves to perform for his crowd
Who is always cheery and loud
The people adore him
He does not bore them
While he jumps up and acts like he's proud.
He never wore a frown
He never wanted to look down
But later that came to an end
When Billy had to bend.
But Billy let that pass
Because he always acts first-class
And all over the world
He had a message to send!!!

Morgan E. Wehmer

Santa Claus ornaments
Christmas angels on the tree
Gingerbread snowmen
Rudolph the red-nosed reindeer
I think Christmas is snowy

Brady T. Wade
Age: 9

SNOWFLAKE

Snowflakes are cold and white
In the hand and from the eye it feels just right

If all the snowflakes stick together
it feels like a gentle, cool blanket

When it melts it feels wet
The pretty forms float to the ground
Too much can make a mound

It shines in a special way like the perfect thing
It almost looks like a diamond ring

It is a sign of Christmas and happiness
It feels like the world is blessed.

Shefali Shah

G ood
R un around with me
A lways there for me
N ice
D arling
P roud of me
A rtistic
R esponsible
E xtraordinary
N eat
T errific
S uper

Luis Gonzalez
Age: 8

G reat and generous
R espect and responsible
A wesome
N ice
D elightful
P erfect
A lways there for me.
R espectful
E xciting
N eat
T errific
S pecial

Jessica Vasquez

THE DOCTOR APPOINTMENT

I was in the ear doctor's big black leather chair.
Its microscopes looking like the arms
of a big mechanical spider.
Sitting there I feel the nervousness and the anxiety
of not knowing what he will do next.
He talks to me telling me
he will do something to help me.
But after going through these ear problems all my life
and having all of the surgeries not work
I begin really doubting my problems
ever can be solved here at this place.
So as he's gone getting his supplies
I feel some sort of fear come over me
but not the usual fear it's like I'm just a guinea pig
in one of their new experiments
like I'm all alone by myself
no one understands what it's like for me
going through these surgeries,
having them not work or what I'm going through.
Some time before the doctor returns to my room
I start calming down.
But just as he enters the room with his assistant
I suddenly feel scared again.
Mostly because I don't know if what he will do
will hurt or not.
It just so happened that it was painful like burning
because that's just what they did.
Then I left the doctor's office
and I was happy because it was over.

Mathew Rogers
Age: 14

SENSES

There's a blackbird singing in the dead of night;
Can't you hear him calling?

There's a wolf howling at the moon tonight;
Can't you hear his cry?

There's an owl looking at you and me;
Can't you see her eyes?

There's a shadow on the windowpane;
Can't you feel the vibe?

There's someone here who loves you so;
Can't you say, "Me, too"?

Just as there's a little boy blue and a man in the moon,
Someone will love you,
Someone will love you,
You better believe that's true.

Nikki Troyer
Age: 12

LITTLE FLAKES OF SNOW

Little flakes of snow falling all around.
I love the snow falling all around the ground.
So come snow, come all day long.
Look I caught one on my tongue.

Joshua Starke

C ookies
H aving fun
R eindeer
I cicles
S anta Claus
T o go caroling
M aking a snowman
A ll people love Christmas
S hopping for winter clothes

Lauren Tillman

DIVORCE

Weeks and weeks go by.
When will it ever stop?
The arguing.
When will the world stop spinning around my head?
What is it all about?
They send me downstairs.
My parents.
Even when the TV is turned up all the way
I can still hear them.
Is this really what it's like?
My parents are getting a divorce.
I want to run far, faraway from here.
My house.
I can't.
The problems will just build up.
My brother's tears running down his small face,
Makes it even harder to deal with.
My parents are getting a divorce.
Time after time they try and try.
But it just won't work.
It wasn't meant to be.
Finally the day draws near
for the final decision to be made.
It's over.
There is no more family.
No happy foursome.
Only four, individual lives.

Everything has and will change.
It'll make me stronger more independent.
But it'll always be embroidered in my heart.
Every time I think about it I weep,
My body weeps.
  For the things I once had.
For the things I'll never have.
The things that still mean so much to me.
It'll never be the same.
It's my parents' divorce.

A new, Beginning.

Kelsey Cataldo
Age: 13

READING

I
love to read
along with friends in school
in the sunny day
so it will get me away from other things.

Joshua Allen McNeal

I stare at my grandma's grave

silent

Unable to speak
My throat is clogged
I want to cry   but tears won't come
We sing songs   but I am still silent
My thoughts boil inside of me

She is in Heaven!

What does Jesus look like?

What's it like Grandma?

I think of
Her laugh
Her smell
Today my grandma is gone
But then again   Today my grandma is home.

Ashley Windbigler
Age: 13

DO YOU REMEMBER...

I can remember the first time
You went fishing with me

I always caught so many
You were busy helping me

Remember when we picked mushrooms
I wouldn't take a bite

Remember when we collected the eggs
I'd drop them with a CRACK...

I still remember all of the times
we spent together

But now you're gone Grandpa
and I hope you're up in Heaven

Amanda Hill

'TWAS THE NIGHT BEFORE OZ FEST

'Twas the night before Oz Fest
I could not sleep
Not a sound in the house
Not even a peep.

When I finally fell asleep
I was dreaming
The sound of music
And everyone screaming.

When I'm awake
I get out of bed
I put on some clothes
And butter my bread.

We get in a car
Dad puts it in drive
I was so excited
I never felt more alive.

When we got there
It was great
It was so fun
There was nothing to hate.

The Oz Fest is
The greatest thing
Bands on stage
And everyone singing.

When we're riding home
I could not hear
Riding home with my dad
There was nothing to fear.

When I got home
I was so wired
I ran around the house
Not a single bit tired.

At quarter to two
I got a bit tired
I got in bed
Now I'm not wired.

When I awake
I take a knife
I butter my bread and tell my dad
That was the greatest day of my life.

Patrick McMahon

SADIE

The first time I saw her she had just been born
Her eyes were closed and she looked like a wet rat.
Her mom was licking her.
Anna handed her to me so I could hold her.

She snuggled against my palm.
My mom and dad said no; we can't get her.
A dog is a big responsibility.
No matter how much we begged they wouldn't budge.

Two weeks later we visited them again.
They had gotten bigger.
We played with them in the whelping box.
   There was
      one brown
         four yellow
            and three black.

They were named after Snow White
and the seven dwarfs.
My mom and dad said no a dog is a big responsibility.
No matter how much we begged they wouldn't budge.

Five of the puppies had been picked.
She was left.
Four weeks later we visited them again.
Their eyes and ears were open
and their personality was showing.
They were growing so fast!
Seven of the puppies were spoken for.
She was left.

My mom and dad said no; a dog is a big responsibility.
No matter how much we begged they wouldn't budge.
A week later all the puppies were spoken for.
She had a home and was being picked up
on Christmas Eve.
On Christmas Eve after church
we went to look at Christmas lights.

Mom put a box in my hand.
In it was a whistle.
Think about it, she said.

She is whistle trained.
We noticed that we were by the McCracken's house.
We screamed for joy.
Abby and I ran in and surprised Anna.
Anna cried, I cried, Abby cried, our moms cried.

Sadie's home was our home.
Mom and Dad
had said
yes.

Brianne Suckow
Age: 14

My birthday is in the snowy cold month of December,
the day right after Christmas Day.
With all the hustle and bustle around Christmastime,
my birthday goes by in a blink of an eye.
I get presents for Christmas and then for my birthday,
but have to wait a whole year before it is time again.
Don't get me wrong I like my birthday,
but if I could change it,
oh how I wish I could change the day of my birthday.
I would change it to a warm bright summer day
when the flowers are blooming
and the sky is a beautiful light blue sky
with big white fluffy clouds.

Caitlin Warrick

COCO THE PUP

Coco the puppy,
As brown as a chocolate bar.
He loved to run near and far.
He was a roly-poly little fellow,
That pranced and danced with each step.
He loved to play and run away.
The cats were in fear as he was near.
Some would call him Coo Coo
But we just call him Coco.

Nikohl Krouser

SUMMER

The sun is shining
All day the birds are chirping
During a warm, hot day.

John Parakowski

FALL AT OXBOW PARK

I feel the bark on the trees,
And see leaves falling upon a slight autumn breeze.
Roaring trains and birds chirping,
Deer tracks hidden in the morning dew.
The scent of pine trees in the air,
I wait for crickets to chirp their last prayers.

Chris Chaffee

A TRUE DANCER

Tutus, makeup, and girls dressed in pink,
when one contemplates dance, that is all they think.
The essential characteristics
lie in poise, beauty, and grace.
A dancer's beaming smile
hides the excruciating pain she must face.
A dancer must not show the endless practices,
Nazi teachers, or muscles she tore;
To make her movements look simple
is what every dancer strives for.
Her legs quiver and her muscles burn.
I can tell she was born to dance
as I watch her passionately turn.
A dancer must be determined, forbearing,
and competitive,
In order for her dancing efforts to be lucrative.
A dancer's need, passion, and love for dance
can be seen in a performance so short,
But one must be a disciplined dancer
to really appreciate the sport.
A true dancer must give herself as a whole
As dance requires body, mind, and soul.

Erin Hendricks
Age: 15

HALLOWEEN

Do you hear ghosts and witches
He, he, ha, ha, ha
Whoooooo!
It's the g, g, g, g, ghost
BOO!
ahhhh

The children ran in the house
BOOM!
DING-DONG
The bell rang.

Nathan Patrick
Age: 9

JUNIOR HIGH

Complicated
Very new
A different world
Much harder than elementary
A growing year for kids
Sometimes hard or difficult
Much is expected
Limited fun
Junior high

Lindsey Manninen

TEACHERS

They work hard
They write a lot
They think millions
With more millions
They probably think
5 million times a day
So they would think
1825 million times a year
Isn't that a lot of
Thinking for a year?

Karen Miller
Age: 11

ONCE I HAD A MEAN OLD CAT

Once I had a mean old cat,
He never sat on my lap;
Instead he scratched everyone he saw,
And my mom and dad didn't like him at all.

We got a dog,
In the fall.
Gulp.
After that I never saw the cat at all.

Nathanael Paul Rich

FALLING SNOW

How can anyone
not like
snow
WHAT
You don't like
snow,
but, but
not even when
it's falling
falling
falling
d
o
w
n

Greta Slabach
Age: 10

ICE CREAM

Ice cream
Sweet, good,
Chocolate, mixed,
Yummy in my tummy.
Ice cream is so good.
Yummy, yummy, ice cream.

Cecily Jones

BOOKS

Books, books, books
I love books
Books, books, books
Some people hate 'em
But I love 'em
Books, books, books
All around the world
Why do people hate 'em
Some are sad
Some are scary
Some are love stories
Some are boring
Most are great
Go and read some more
It's great to read
So why do people hate 'em
'Cause I love 'em
Books, books, books
Books from Ireland, from Europe
Great books bad books
Some people hate 'em but not me

Christopher Heinrich
Age: 10

LAKE MICHIGAN

See the glittering blue water in the lake.
Feel the rocks as you walk on them along the shore.
Smell the fresh crisp air.
Hear the ferries as they move swiftly through the lake.
See the green grass shining in the sunlight.
All this makes me feel God is here.

Adib Behrouzi
Age: 8

LOST

My dog is lost, what should I do?
I last saw him chewing my shoe.
I got real mad and kicked him out.
Oh, how I wish I'd see his snout.

I'll put up signs, posters, and more
'Til I see him come through my door.
But until then I'll have to say,
"Never again will I send him away."

Emily Koontz

SAND

As quick as my little toes touched
                    they were pulled away

    The oven-baked sand
                    burned my small toes

I wanted to run into the water
                    to feel that cool feeling

            But

Mom said not to run on the sand
                    my toes felt as though
                                    they were burning off

        I still wanted toes!

    If I didn't have toes
        ...I don't know what I would do

        so

    I RAN!

        As fast as my tiny legs
                        would go

Mom was yelling for me to stop
                    but I had to keep running

I was almost there
I finally made it

To the icy,
refreshing,
water

When I viewed my surroundings
I realized

I was in the ocean!

Kayla Leiter
Age: 14

I'M NOT

I'm not crazy.
I'm not lazy.
I'm not loud.
I'm not a cloud.
I'm not graceful.
I'm not helpful.
I'm not mean.
I'm not keen.
I'm not a tree.
I'm just well me.

Kati Jeanette Spite

111

NATURE

Nighttime silence.
The wind, softly turning in the air,
The owl, trying to ask who is there,
The raccoons, scattering down the tree getting water,
The bluebirds, resting in their nest.

They are all saying that nighttime is the best.

So nature, when daytime's here,
Bring out the flowers and spring cheer,
Because when daytime's over,
Nighttime lasts for hours.

So all those people will see
That daytime might be happy,
But nighttime's truly the best.

Katelyn Hill

HALLOWEEN WEEKEND

We went up to my lake
on Halloween weekend
to have a little fun
to play a little trick on my friend
we got him good
he didn't like clowns
so we scared him
he was freaked out of his mind
until he realized it was us
he was really mad
but we all gathered and took a picture.

Ryan Hurstel
Age: 13

MY MONSTER

My monster is way too slimy.
   It even smells a little too limey.
My monster tries to be nice.
   But I think it might need some sugar and spice.
My monster wears a big red bow.
   I even think it goes a little too slow.
My monster sheds a lot of tears.
   It even has big pointy ears.
My monster makes a mess everywhere.
   Oh I wish it would just go somewhere!

Lindsay Syson

SNOWBELLS

Snowbells ring in the hills
And the snow gives them fills
Ring ding-a-ling ring-ding
Hear the snowbells sing

All around I hear them sound
Christmastime is almost found
Snowbells on the sleigh
Hear the pretty horse neigh
Through the bills and up to town
Christmas will never make anybody frown
Snowbells ring when Santa comes
Carolers will sing with lots of hums.

Katelyn Petrovich

ALL-AMERICAN HEARTS

The hearts of Americans are filled with truth and love
Our hearts are filled with courage and with that
we stand tall for our beloved country
I am proud to say that I am an American
We will fight 'til we can fight no more
and we will be proud that we saved our country
and that we risked our lives for it
and we thank our brave soldiers for that
I am proud to be an American!

Paige Thompson

MY CLUB

I skate up a tree,
Into my club.
My club is a mess,
And I do not clean it up.
I just sit in my club.
I should call it Club Mess!

Zachary Anglemyer

OUR TWO RATS

We have two rats,
  They can be brats.
They hide in a broom,
  In a big room.
They stay in a cage,
  But never get a page.
They may be white,
  But they're not a sight.
They have big feet,
  But they don't look like a beet.
They have bald tails,
  But they aren't rails.
They have red eyes,
  But they don't look like pies.
They eat food,
  If they aren't in a bad mood.

Brittany Robinson
Age: 10

DOGS

I like dogs
They jump over logs.
Some live in a house
Some might chase a mouse.
They like food
They can be in a bad mood.
You might have to clean up
They can eat out of a cup.
They might not wear hats
They can be little brats.
If they're brats
They chase cats.

Zack Harlan
Age: 10

There was a cricket named Bob
Who got fired from his job.
He couldn't believe it
So he had to leave it
And then he started to sob.

Brittany Treash

HALLOWEEN

Scream
Boohoo
He, he, he
A ghost
One of
The kids say I
Hear a
Boom
Went a
Crumble, Clang, Clang
Scream went
One of
The kids
Ha, ha, ha
Went the
Ghost
Hovering
In front of them
Then the
Ghost chased
The kids out
Of the
Creepy castle

Cole Love
Age: 9

Hardship is
like climbing
a mountain
forever

Chris Martin

MY DOG NAMED NANCY

My dog named Nancy, she is fancy.
She lives in the tub.
She plays all day and night.
When I take a bath she is in the tub.
Nancy likes nasty food.
She wets the bed and my mom thinks I did it.

Monica J. Jeffrey

WILL THE DARKNESS END

The darkness looms,
Filling every room with glooms,
Shadows on the wall,
Creeping people make things fall,
Doors creak,
Dogs sneak,
Silence consumes the air,
Filling everyone with despair,
Outside thunder claps,
Against the windows rain slaps...

Yet hope remains,
Like a stain,
As a single candle glows,
Through all hope flows,
For all remembered,
The darkness doesn't last forever,
Soon the storm will be gone,
And the power back on,
So they all sleep tight,
Through the pitch-black night.

Julie Middaugh
Age: 16

WHITE AND RED, THE COLORS OF AMERICA

To the left of her is a short, impatient man,
she looks down to him and laughs.
The sky is black,
a full moon hiding.
Lights flash on beautiful faces,
her smile goes unnoticed.
The city cars scream to her,
but she does not listen.
She reads the minds of all that pass,
hoping someone would notice.

In her apartment she sits,
everything and empty white.
Silently she makes her dinner,
eating slowly, without thought.
She goes to the couch,
reads the daily paper.
Behind her is the only picture,
a white magnolia.
Tired of their laughter and glee,
she stole it from the wall of her only neighbor.

She was very proud of this,
it made her feel normal.

She sat up straight,
staring at the paper.
Merely raising an eyebrow,
at the screams that began in the neighbor's apartment.

The thief's bullet missed the screaming man,
went through her neighbor's wall,
and into her head,
turning the magnolia behind her red.

Amanda Jo Williams
Age: 15

If I was a knight of King Arthur's long ago
The stories I could tell
About the battles I've been in
Where I fought well
Beside the knights of the Round Table
With my sword

Tyler Vermillion

Since it is fall,
My brother starts football.
And since my brother is too small,
He will need to wait 'til he's tall.

Lauren Alwine
Age: 9

PRETTY PERSON

You pretty person, please be mine, you are so fine.
Your house smells like lime,
your smile is like diamonds shining,
and your voice is like chimes ringing.
You are so very kind and have a clean mind.
I hope you find me you pretty person.
  Please be mine.

James Michael Tapocsi

I HAVE PROBLEMS

I have problems...
I always seem to be doing something wrong,
My mom said to eat my plums,
But I just sang.

My friends at school tell me to run,
Instead I go to the swings
My teacher said to write about the sun,
Instead I wrote about wings.

My gym teacher said to reach for your toes,
Instead I went and took a nap,
My music teacher said to reach for your toes,
But I put my instrument in my lap.

My teacher said to sharpen my lead,
But I read about Rome
My mom said to go to bed,
But I went in the living room to finish this poem.

Samantha Barnett
Age: 10

THE WATERFALL

See the dew and the sparkles
On the beautiful waterfall.
Leaves around the trees.
See the mist coming off the waterfall.
Smell the fresh grapes.
Feel the wet dew on your feet.
Taste the good water.
Hear the birds singing.
Thank God for this place.

Angela Kramer
Age: 8

HALLOWEEN

Oooooooo
Went the ghost
Ahaaaa
Went the people
Eeek
Went the mouse
He he he he ha ha ha ha
Went the witch
And scared the mouse and ghost
And people away.

Brittney Garza

POTATO CREEK

Look at the lake, a shimmering backdrop for the trees.
Observe trees that are autumn colors.
Orange, red, and yellow are seen.
Glimpse a snake slithering across the wide path.
Notice its light gray color.
Cormorants fly low and then dive like arrows
   into the water.
Hear the huge bass jump and splash up
   out of the clear water.
It falls back in like a rock.
This hike is like looking at a painting designed by God.

Edward J. Hunckler
Age: 9

MY FRIEND BOB

I have a friend named Bob
He likes to be in a mob
He has a mouse
That lives in the house
He has a snake
That lives in a lake

Kenneth Dean Baugher

CHRISTMASTIME

Christmastime is almost here
It's my favorite time of year
I get clothes, books, and stuffed bears
But we shouldn't really care
Because Christmas is about a little boy
This little boy is named Jesus
We should not need presents to please us
Because Christmas is really about Jesus
Christmas is also about our family
Of whom we care deeply about
This is what Christmas is really about

Janelle Pyclik
Age: 12

HAWAII

See the reflection of the sky off the clean blue water.
Feel the rocky sand under your feet.
Hear the ocean waves crashing against the shore.
Watch the sharp shells while you put on your lotion.
Smell the slimy sunscreen on your arms.
Makes me feel God is near.

Adam Rhody

TEENAGE WORLD

I feel unwanted, uninvited, unaccepted
in this world.
I feel as if everyone is staring at me,
like I don't belong,
like I'm different.
I feel that just because I've changed my ways,
that I am now considered weird.
Why is this teenage world such torture?
You try to be yourself and you get criticized.
I'm on the verge of tears every day.
Sure I have good times,
What's that anyways?
I just laugh one minute,
and cry the next.
I'm so stressed out and tired,
I zone out all day.
I try my hardest; yet I'm still
unwanted, uninvited, unaccepted.
I feel so misunderstood.

Brandy N. Purnell

LAKE WAWASEE

See the geese floating gently in the dirty lake.
Smell the seaweed laying on the sandy shore.
Feel the cool breeze blowing against my face.
Hear the motorboats moving slowly in the water.
See the waves ripple back and forth.
Makes me feel God is near.

Rachel Nickerson

CATS

I have six cats
They wear silly hats
They sleep on my bed
They really like to shed.

Sandra J. Culler

School is near,
now school is here.
I like school all year,
School is here, let's cheer!

Gabrielle Skwarcan
Age: 8

HALLOWEEN

Halloween
Halloween, night
Carve the pumpkin
A creepy, dark moon
Spooky

Julia Hendricks

WHIRL OF EMOTIONS

I still cannot believe what you did to me
Your acts were so cruel that you just could not see
I endured the pain for such a long time
Yet when we were with each other, I acted fine
I wanted our relationship to immediately end
You had said things to me that would never mend
I began to tell you how I felt, but started crying
I was just so tired of all your lying
But I decided to give you another try
Thinking, that things would fix as time passed by
But things only got worse
I felt as if I were cursed
You said that there was nothing between you and her
But as you spoke, all I heard was a blur
It was hard to say good-bye to you
But I am starting to see someone new
Now my heart is starting to heal
Yet never quite sure of how I should feel
I am beginning to be so strong
A feeling I haven't felt in so long

Chelsey Hayden
Age: 16

ALL IN A BIG CITY

Cars rush by,
An aluminum mass on a smooth black sheet.
Always in a hurry, back and forth,
Each in each other's way.
Almost a blur of odor against gray skies.
All in a big city.

Sounds blurring, weaving between passersby.
Lights blinding, twinkling,
Glowing in the blanket-like sky.
Sights of intimidating museums, fragrant restaurants,
Chic art galleries.
All in a big city.

People with brightly colored clothes and crazy fashions
    walk by.
Classy people, fashionable people, rich people,
Poor people.
A swirl of bodies parted like the sea by only the roads.
Laughing, talking, walking,
Jamming to an invisible rhythm.
All in a big city.

The thrill, the air of excitement,
The mannerisms ever surprising,
The amazement found all in a big city.

Hannah Osborn

SCHOOL

School is a place we go to learn.
A place we take our turn.
A place where we have some fun.
And make new friends with everyone.

Randy Kulesia
Age: 8

CAT

My neighbor's name is Candy
She has a cat named Randy
He is so fat
He doesn't look like a cat
But they all think he is dandy.

Derrick Beatty

SCHOOL DURING FALL

Another school during the fall
   I can't wait to play football.
I sit and stare at the clock
   As it goes ticktock ticktock.
The work we do is very hard
   Not like making a birthday card.
Finally the work time ends
   I get to play with my friends

Calvin Zielinski
Age: 8

OTTAWA NATIONAL FOREST

See the glistening lake
   with shining, shimmering fish in its deep blue waters.
Smell the fragrance of the dark green fir trees.
Feel the fast-moving lake
   as its cold water moves through your toes.
Hear the wind as it softly blows
   through the towering trees.
When I got to Ottawa National Forest
   my soul feels very content.

Margaret Pendergast

Olivia,
you see me
on my knees
crying, because you left me.
People tell me
you're watching over me
and loving me.
I love you too.
You're happy now,
because the suffering's
stopped.
No more tubes
stuck into you.
Now you can walk
and you can talk,
hear with no fear.
You have me crying every day
I can't do anything right.
I just want to
hold you tight.
All day long you'll be
in the biggest part of my heart.
I hope you'll save
a spot for me up there,
but for now I'll be down here.

Briana Dawson

From the top of the trees,
there are leaves.
The leaves fall down,
down to the ground.
In the leaves you run
and have fun.

Leaves turn red, purple, orange and gold
but also, fall is cold.

Kandyse Kaizer
Age: 9

School is near, school is here,
Autumn's the best time of the year!
It's when all the leaves turn brown,
Then they fall to the ground.
I found many leaves on the ground,
After that they formed a mound,
When I jumped in the leaves, it made a sound.

Rebecca Latson
Age: 9

LOVE

Love is a box of chocolate.
Love is the month of February.
Love is the season of spring.
Love is the song of happiness.
Love is the touch of a heart-shaped box.
Love is the memory
    of when my baby brother named Ryan was born.

Danielle Lappan
Age: 5

FLORIDA

Smell the fish-like scent.
Hear the sound of water crashing against the shore!
See the clouds like giant cotton balls.
Feel the hot sand on your feet.
See the warm sun rising in the sky.
I love this place because God made it.

Thomas Cook Jr.
Age: 8

THE CHANGING COLORS OF FALL

Hear the wind blow.
See the grass wave, as the air sweeps across it.
Watch the green leaves turn different colors
   as fall approaches.
Hear the raindrops come down and pelt the dry leaves.
I love the fall.
The sounds and beauty make me relax.

Shane Singleton
Age: 9

TREES, TREES, TREES

Trees don't carry keys,
Trees don't eat peas,
Trees don't have knees,
Trees don't have fleas,
Trees can't move about with ease,
But trees DO understand the word
PLEASE.

Sara Elizabeth Buyer
Age: 9

MY DOG

My dog, Macs, is a puppy who is black
he understands German
We say "Yets" he understands
we say "Ous" he knows perfectly in German language
nice
feisty
little puppy, not little anymore he's Big!

Victoria Maclain
Age: 10

FALL

Fall is near. Fall is here.
It's the best time of the year.
The leaves are falling.
The geese are leaving because winter is coming.
Thanksgiving is in fall too.
It's when your family comes to visit you.

Ashley N. Miller
Age: 10

FRIENDS

Friends are forever,
   Friends 'til the end
Expressing your feelings
   Whether they're good or bad
Sleepovers and secrets,
   Laughing and crying
We're friends forever,
   Friends 'til the end!

Melissa Gingerich
Age: 11

HORSES

Horses eat hay
They don't say hay.
Horses don't pay bills.
Horses like to play on hills
Horses can neigh
But horses can obey!

Katelin Marie VanMeter
Age: 9

IT APPEARS TO BE

It appears to be rough
It appears to be tough
It appears to be dark
It appears as a mark
It appears to be dries
It appears to be cries
It appears to be crafty
It appears to be drafty
It appears to be rain
"Through all my pain."

Jessenia DeLaPaz

FALL

Fall is a good time of the year,
With leaves here and there
Of all colors, leaves from the trees,
Leaves all the way up to your knees,
Rake them up into a pile and jump in,
The leaves go in the air,
And go back down to the ground.
Oh what fun!

Zachary Riley
Age: 10

THE BATTLE

The battle was long and hard.
But the troops kept fighting on.
For they were brave and they had faith,
and were not let down.
For some were hurt and scarred,
and others were not harmed.
But the unharmed were lucky.
For I have no reason for battle!

Brian Joseph Pilla

I HATE MY ARM

I hate my arm
And animals on a farm.
I hate fish in the sea
And stinging bumblebees
But most of all
I hate the tree house that broke my arm!

Jasmine Nicole Baker
Age: 9

My school is tall,
When I am so small.
My desk is so big
That on its top I can dance to the jig.

Casarah Glover
Age: 9

I HOLD IN MY HANDS

I hold in my hands the uniqueness of me,
I look around,
I see the town,
But no one is like me,
There is no one with the same brown hair
and brown eyes,
No one with the same freckles,
No one could ever try to be me,
Because in the end no one, I mean no one is just like me!

Chelsea A. Graf
Age: 10

THE NIGHT WHEN I FIGHT!

There is a bad night
  When my brother and I fight!
My body got so hot,
  I burned my cot
My brother threw a ball at me.
  I've got a big bruise as you can see.

Alexander Keith Jackson
Age: 8

BUGS!

I hate bugs,
They hide in old tubs,
They hide under rugs
One time I saw some on a dead mouse
So I patched up the holes in my house
But I forgot to patch up one hole
Here come the bugs!!!

Tommy Billings
Age: 9

Leaves fall
from trees so tall.
Flowers die
and I start to cry;
then I recall
here comes fall.

Iara Ibay

My sister is a scaredy-cat!
  My sister is a scaredy-cat!
She's afraid of a braid.
  She's scared to go to the arcade.
When she goes to bed.
  She hits her head.
She needs the light to say good night.
  One more thing when it's light she flies a kite.

Rebecca L. Gutierrez
Age: 8

SCHOOL IS COOL!

School is cool.
We like to learn things
like science, social studies, math, English
and last but not least reading.
School is fun also.
I love school.

Melinda Louise Wyrick

MICKEY'S AND MINNIE'S FLOODED HOUSE

Mickey Mouse!!! Mickey Mouse!!!
Your house flooded high!!
When I look at it I can almost die!!!
Minnie Mouse!!! Minnie Mouse!!!
Look what happened to your house!
It is flooded as tall as your blouse!!

Andriana Danielle Gonzalez
Age: 8

DONNEL LAKE

Look at the sparkling waters
  and travel down a two-mile stream.
See the beautiful fish
  and cranes picking berries with their huge beaks.
Turtles pop up everywhere while you enter another lake.
  The sweet-smelling air makes me remember
God is near.

Adam Keszei

A WEIRD CHRISTMAS

Christmas is fun Christmas is cold.
I even got something old.
Once my brother even got coal with a mole.
He threw the coal out and kept the mole.
He named the mole Lowell.
And his mole got to go to a hole.
His mole was so smart he could read a scroll.

Jacob E. Johnson
Age: 9

The cookies are great.
Santa is sledding today.
Santa Claus is cool.

Jacob Wyman
Age: 9

I. U. BASKETBALL

Tom Coverdale
leader, red hair
rebounding, shooting, scoring
number three, high scorer, coach, black suit
inspiring, teaching, planning
strategic, intelligent
Coach Mike Davis

Gregory T. Kolodziej
Age: 10

I love you
I love you
I love you divine
Give me a kiss, I'll give you a dime.

Brittany Carter

THIS IS THE WAY
MY FOSTER GRANDPARENT TALKS

This is the way my foster grandparent talks
To hear about my day
And says things that are really funny
Or to help me when I am stuck on a problem
Then says that I am doing a good job
This is the way my foster grandparent talks.

Christina Greenidge

MY BIKE

Riding my bike,
with the wind in my hair,
it feels like I'm flying in the air,
wondering if I'll EVER get there!
OH MY! Is there a rest stop anywhere?

Serjio Felipe Flores

CHEROKEE LANDS

I take a step onto Cherokee lands
Once sacred and loved
Now polluted and scarce with food
Now withering and hated
I can see the footsteps of what might be a Cherokee's
I see where the woodpecker pecked
Where the Cherokee stepped
All the memories left

Harrison J. Wagner

JELLY BROTHER

Once my brother ate a jellybean
and turned into a jelly brother!
Me and my mother had to make peanut butter!
Anyone got bread and MILK?

Adam R. Koziol

DON'T GO DOING DRUGS!

Don't go doing drugs they are bad for you and me.
But if you do you will feel really bad.
You will feel really yucky too.
It will be all because you're drunk.
People can get hurt all because of you.
So let me tell you this.
Don't go doing drugs.
Now please take my advice.

Clairanne Porter
Age: 8

SNOWFLAKES

Snowflakes,
   Snowflakes,
      Everywhere.
Falling here
   Falling there.
Hooray!
  The snow is here!!!

Emily Rollins

THE TWO LITTLE PENGUINS

Two little penguins lived by the ice.
One of the penguins liked to eat hot, fresh spice.

One day the penguins had tons of lice
So they took a bath in the water twice.

One day their mother penguin made a great apple pie,
The penguins ate so much that their stomachs had a sigh.

Fariha Khan
Age: 10

SITTING HERE

With leaves all around me
On the wet ground
Behind, tall weeds hide me
Near a lot of trees
Outside is cold
Since no one is here it is peaceful
Without any noise but the wind howling
And the birds singing
Above me the sun shines bright
Below me is cold brown soil
During this time I miss talking to the animals
Before me are colorful leaves
Beyond me are bare forests
Off to the fire I go.

Brianne K. Burkhart
Age: 11

AUTUMN IS GREAT

Autumn looks like colorful leaves falling.
Autumn feels like wind rushing on your face.
Autumn sounds like whistling winds.
Autumn tastes like turkey coming out of the oven.
Autumn smells like fresh apple pie.

Gabby Savieo

NIGHT SOUNDS OF MERRY LEA

Silent things are:
The cold empty night
Frozen hard mud grabbing our shoes
Tall cattail grass by the swampy lake
Loud things are:
Turkeys gobbling for their food
Wind whistling through the trees
People laughing while writing poems
Eternal things are:
Memories from spending the night
Poetry scrapbooks from Merry Lea
Beautiful scenery by the lake

Shawn Kelley
Age: 11

FALL

Fall looks like beautiful trees,
twirling leaves, wobbly trees.
Fall feels like icy cold winds,
twirling winds, tornado winds.
Fall sounds like whistling winds,
crunchy leaves, howling winds.
Fall tastes like fresh sweet pumpkin pie,
delicious apple cider.
Fall smells like fresh sweet Thanksgiving.

Ashlee N. Wakeman

MY OWN, SPECIAL SPOT

Beyond the stone soup firepit,
Past the barn,
Next to the animals,
Below everyone else,
Over the mud,
Through the trees,
Before the pavilion,
On the ground,
With the rocks,
In the dirt,
Is my own, special spot.

Kelsey Shanabarger
Age: 11

MERRY LEA

Merry Lea was so much fun
It's really sad that it's all done
The best part about it was having fun with my friends
But my unforgettable memories will never end
We roasted marshmallows and sang songs all night
Nothing gave me a bit of fright
And like I said, Merry Lea was so much fun
It's really sad that it's all done

Brianna Nicole Wheaton

LEAVES OF RED AND GOLD

There was an autumn leaf
of red and gold
Floating gently very gently
to the ground.
Then with other leaves
swirling 'round and 'round.
Running swiftly
on the street
All around
the people's feet,
and when they slow
on top of a lawn
a rake comes down
and herds them
like a colored wave!
Safely tied
in a plastic sack
they sadly fear
and know,
they will not be
coming back!

Anna Grace O'Dell
Age: 10

FIREWORKS

It's night in the city
Brilliant colors fill the sky
Explosions are heard.

Julia M. Crant

RED JO

Funny
little, playful
jumping, running, charging
rest then fall asleep the whole day
Puppy

Kelsy Listenberger
Age: 10

MY DOG

My dog is gray
And she likes to play
She is always alert
She helps you when you are hurt.

Stephanie Nifong
Age: 11

THE BIRD

one warm sunny day
I saw a chirping jay
it looked so beautiful
sitting there by the bay

Robert Pope
Age: 9

CATCHING STARS

Every Saturday night I sit on the edge of my bed
catching stars thinking of what I should do the next day
then I start thinking of YOU

Dedicated to my parents Rick and Shellie

Sommer Donielle Peyton

A DAY

The sun
Shining the day through
Following you everywhere
Disappears at dusk

The moon
Shining the night through
Following you everywhere
Disappears at dawn

Melissa Bucker
Age: 10

CHRISTMAS

Snow is falling from very high.
Down, down, down it falls from the sky.
After Santa leaves in his sleigh
All the boys and girls come out and play.

Lindsey Micucci

KISSIPOO!

In the car
Waiting to go to Wal-Mart
  Crash!
We got hit
Nobody hurt
The funny part was
They were boyfriend and girlfriend
They were kissing!
Sick!

Brooke Carter
Age: 9

I like Santa Claus.
I like Rudolph the reindeer.
I like Santa's sleigh.

Jacob Doppler
Age: 8

ANIMALS!!

Elephants are super strong
and their trunks are very long.
Fish, they swim everywhere
and when I go fishing I'll catch one, I swear!
Monkeys swing from branch to branch
and cause a monkey avalanche.
They like to leap from limb to limb
but sometimes... they fall!

Harrison M. Sade
Age: 9

RAINBOW

All rainbows are in the sky
They have shiny colors
They are so colorful.
The colors look like colorful books.

Valeria Perez
Age: 10

FALL

Fall looks like beautiful two-toned trees.
Fall feels like chilly winds and crunchy leaves.
Fall sounds like whistling howling winds.
Fall tastes like family dinners.
Fall smells like burning leaves

Shelby T. Gillenwater

RAIN

Outside a cloud covers the sun
And the cloud is big and black.
I like the rain!
I like the rain!
Man it stopped!

Robert Kadisak
Age: 8

FALL

Fall looks like pretty leaves
and very windy whistling and howling
and yummy peppermint ice-cream pie
and burning leaves and Thanksgiving dinner.

Victoria Wert

JAKE

Jake and his snake
Went to rake
To find his friend Ben
And Jake found a hen
To stop the cake.

Jacob Koartge
Age: 13

FALLTIME

Fall looks like flaming leaves
Fall feels like hard stormy winds
Fall sounds like whistling winds
Fall tastes like creamy ice cream
Fall smells like apple cider

Cliff Crabill

THE DAY

The day we will play will be full of hay.
We will play in the hay all day, okay?

Rachel Schnitzer
Age: 8

FALL

Fall looks like beautiful leaves on trees.
Fall feels like hard winds blowing.
Fall sounds like crunching leaves.
Fall tastes like turkey.
Fall smells like pumpkin pie.

Emily Ditton

MILLENNIUM FORCE

Waiting in line with an hour to go,
Hoping that our nervousness would not show,
Now here we are going up the hills,
Of one of the biggest and fastest thrills.

Tyler Koors

SINGLE MOUNTAINS

Farewell my beautiful mountains,
for tomorrow we shall awaken to nothing as speakable
except peace and silence,
otherwise known as birds chirping,
eagles flapping their wings,
and the wolf's hair shuttering in the summer breeze,
if you ever see such a heartbreaking sight
remember this little poem
it just might help you on your journey ahead.

Victoria Lynn Burch
Age: 9

LOVE

Love tastes like chocolate chip
that my mom makes on Easter morning,
love is the color of strawberries that I pick,
love is a memory of when my mom
tucks me in at night.

Marie Becker

SECRETS

Good secrets are like a box of whispers
murmuring in happy agreement.
Good secrets taste like yummy, fluffy whipped cream
on strawberries.
I think nice secrets are shaped like cool wisps of wind
in the morning breeze.
Secrets are a memory of many of my friends
that I tell secrets to.
Some secrets dream of being known
to all who wish to know them.
Good and bad secrets feel like breath in your ear.
Both also feel like a lot of mixed-up emotions.

Anna Theresa Polovick

JOY

Joy is a box of happiness.
Joy is a song of greatness.
Joy is the month of December.
Joy is the year 2003.
Joy tastes like a box of cookies.
Joy is a shape of a star.
Joy is a memory of my family.
Joy dreams of good times.
Joy remembers happiness.
Joy is a touch of an angel.
Joy is a dance of friendship.
Joy is summer.
Joy smells like a fresh flower.
Joy has a pocket of sunshine.
Joy sounds like nature's animals.

Kaley Kubiak

FALL LEAVES

Leaves are fun to run and jump and play.
I could stay and play all day.
Let's pile them in a bunch.
And make them crunch and crunch.

Brittney Peregrine
Age: 8

IT'S THANKSGIVING

It's Thanksgiving, Hooray!
We will eat lots today.
I like going to see Grandpa,
because he lives with Grandma.
"Thank you," we say,
on Thanksgiving day.

Staci Jurgonski
Age: 8

AN HOUR OF MY SUMMER

I went out to the beach,
and I had some fun in the sun.
Then I went in the ocean,
which was cool just like the pool.

Stephanie Gardner

Fall is fun for one and all.
The leaves turn brown then they fall.
I pick up the phone to give my friend a call.
We play in the leaves thanks to fall.

Angel Van Dusen
Age: 8

THE EARTH'S WAYS

The earth is cool,
when it has no school.
The earth rocks,
when it has no blocks.
The earth wears a hat,
when it can't play with a cat.
The earth walks,
when it can't talk.
The earth plays,
like a big maze.
The earth plays with a bat,
when it can't find its hat.
The earth gets sad,
when someone is mad.
This is what the earth can do.
How about you?

Sabrina Fujawa

Reading page after page
Hours at a time
Living others' stories of magic, danger, and crime
Last page yet still I want more

Ashley Carroll

LAKE MICHIGAN

Feel the wonderful breeze!
Hear the singing sea gulls.
Feel the crunchy sand under your feet.
See those curving waves crash to the shore.
See the beautiful minnows jumping out of the water.
Hear the speedboats honking madly at one another.
Be thankful for your wonderful God!

Raffaella Stroik
Age: 9

THE JOURNEY OF BUBBLE GUM AND SAPPHIRE

There once was a girl named Bubble Gum.
Who was as skinny as a crumb.
Each day she ate one pea.
That's how she became so tiny.
Bubble Gum also liked monkeys.
She said they reminded her of her Grandma Clonkies.
Bubble Gum had a pet monkey named Sapphire.
Sapphire hated to sit around a campfire.
One time Sapphire saw one,
And started screaming, "Run, run, run."
Bubble Gum's mom got tired of it.
So she shouted, "Make that monkey quit!"
She also said, "Make that monkey a stray."
Bubble Gum got so mad, she decided to run away.
She packed a suitcase full of peas and monkey pictures.
And for some odd reason, she packed cupcake mixtures.
Bubble Gum and Sapphire ran away
to a place called Hackelbestalors.
There they became pro sailors.
The only food they ate was peas and cupcakes.
So now all they have is a really big stomachaches.
Now they are smart and are heading home.
And now I'm going to end this poem.

Emily J. Mastej
Age: 12